How We Found

the Secret Path to True Love

8 men reveal their real life stories on their journey to finding genuine love and happiness

ISBN:0989900924
ISBN-13:978-0989900928
Global Fiance Incorporated, Honomu, HI

Priceless Opportunity for Christian Single Men
Who Are Resolved to Be Successful...

Claim your FREE
INTERNATIONAL ROMANCE
BONUS PACK

jam-packed with everything you need to be
successful this year.

Your FREE GIFT INCLUDES:

1. International Romance Success Workshop Online Access
Experience this once-in-a-lifetime One Day Workshop with Peter
Christopher, author of "How to Meet, Date and Marry Your Filipina
Wife." This access is over a $397 value, complete with video recordings
and workshop downloads. In will help you learn exactly how to go about
online dating and how to plan for a possible trip and relationship.

2. A copy of "How to Meet, Date and Marry Your Filipina Wife"
We'll rush you a copy of Christian Filipina founder Peter Christopher's
ultimate handbook to ensure your safety and success.

3. Free Romance Consultation
Receive a certificate for a complimentary 15-minute consultation with
one of our trained Romance Consultants, to help you answer any
questions you have on your mind:

| IVY | ALVIE | MARILYN | GLAIZA | JARETTE |

There is a one-time charge of $5.95 to cover shipping and handling of your FREE gift.

To claim your free gift, simply call us at 800-578-1469 or go to
www.ChristianFilipina.com/freegift

CONTENTS

"Christian Filipina is based on integrity. You all are doing your utmost to ensure that subscribers get a genuine, legitimate, good experience. I corresponded with others, actually there were so many to choose from, great caliber people."

1

MARLIN & GEMMA GRAHAM

Before They Met

Marlin - Amarillo, Texas, USA

"Doing refrigeration and air conditioning was just routine —
day to day, working, coming home, kinda' feeling detached;
going forward, but feeling that something was lacking in my
life," Marlin remembered. "I wanted a relationship with
someone that is a God-fearing Christian girl. I prayed for God
to give me a mate."

"I believe women have special gifts that God gave them, and
whenever they are combined with someone of the opposite sex
it brings out the best in both of them," said Marlin.

Gemma - Ormoc City, Leyte, Philippines

"I was a working woman, a career woman," said Gemma.

"My life before my husband was my job, and home, and also I was very faithful, so I have so many ministries. I was also active in the church. I made a personal prayer to God and I've been asking for a certain situation and then it happened. Marlin is a Christian."

Their Decision to Search ... and Finding ChristianFilipina.com

Marlin had been married many years before, but at 52, he was ready to settle down with the right woman. He searched the Internet for Christian girls in the Philippines, found the Christian Filipina website and "watched for a while." After about a month he decided, "this one is the best I've found."

Marlin said Christian Filipina is "based on integrity. Y'all doing your utmost to ensure that subscribers get a genuine, legitimate, good experience. I corresponded with others, actually there were so many to choose from, great caliber people. Then I found Gemma's picture and liked her profile so I just went ahead and paid for a membership for one year so we could start chatting back and forth and emailing and so on.

"I narrowed it down to her," Marlin said. "I enjoyed the conversation. She was educated like me. She was involved with the church and being a Christian. I thought that was important."

A Good Christian Girl

At nearly 40 years old, Gemma had never dated before she met Marlin. She was serious about marriage with a true Christian. Gemma said, "I've been with many dating sites. I corresponded with many people as long as they were Christians. The thing about Christian Filipina is I find it very, very, very good." She likes the whole concept of the website: "You're really helping women and you are also helping the men. You have some tips on your website; the information is informative. I am always encouraged by you; you have good Bible verses on your website. I really like that."

Merlin said, "Gemma took care of her mom and went to church and I was going through the same thing, helping out my mom, and so we had common ground there. And she didn't have a big family and I don't either, so I got to know her." Their similarities "just made it more interesting and compelling."

Getting to Know Each Other

In Marlin, Gemma found desirable qualities, including maturity, responsibility and kindness. "Actually he's economy-minded, is very responsible, has a stable job, shows so much concern and is very caring."

Marlin said, "A few weeks before I went to Ormoc I called her and I was surprised by her voice. Her voice was neat and as intriguing as her emails had been. Gemma was the only one I was interested in. I actually prayed about it and felt good about meeting her. I felt that she was a colleague that was put on my heart and so I was confident in that visit. I was more excited to see her in person because I thought her picture didn't do her justice. She looked better in person. I was very, very satisfied and very impressed." Marlin visited Gemma for four weeks and "by the 3rd week I asked her to marry me."

Friendly Philippines

The Philippines is "such a friendly country," said Marlin, who received advice from Filipinos back home "on what to do and where to stay" when he arrived. He also found that once a meaningful relationship is established with a potential partner, "you are an honored guest with her and her friends. They wished the best for her and thought that it would be a good thing for her to be married if it is God's will. They welcomed me with open arms. I was overwhelmed with kindness and love and appreciation. So it was a very pleasant experience."

Immigration and Marriage!

Marlin and Gemma used an attorney to help them process her K-1 fiancée visa. "I thought everything went quickly once you get the paperwork initiated and get it in the system," said Marlin. "It just seemed that once we were at a certain point it just snowballed really quick but it was exciting the whole seven months.

"Ours was a simple wedding," remembered Marlin. "We did it at a church with a preacher and that's what we felt comfortable with because she did not have family members here and my family is very small. That's what worked for both of us. So we got married about three weeks after she was here.

"Things are different" for Gemma in Amarillo, "but she's not more foreign than anybody else to American culture and values and attitudes," said Marlin. "One thing I can say about what really keeps surprising me is we're so much alike rather than not alike. She seems to assimilate well into the community. She's very pleasant to everybody. I'm just really pleased, when she's introduced, at the warmness everybody shows her."

The Future is Exciting!

"I'm very content and excited about the future!" Marlin said. Gemma "keeps a well maintained house and cooks all the time. She's excited about our future because she's never been in the United States, so anything that I think is maybe mundane, she's excited to do. It's really easy to come up with things to do all the time that are fun, like traveling. For me, it's rediscovering the United States, and I like being a tour guide. It's a challenge. Her questions are funny and her observations of America have made me actually aware and more sensitive of the culture we live in. She points out things I've never thought about or noticed.

"It's great to have someone to go to church with, to be a companion, a partner. She's been a very good inspiration to me. She challenges me and helps me to be the best I can be. I think that's their culture. I have a Filipino friend at work, and we're always talking, and he always tells me, 'Well, she's doing that because she's honoring you or respecting you.' Or something she does that I think is really neat is just something that they would do in a marriage."

"It's been quite a privilege to know her and for her to be my wife," concluded Marlin.

2

KEVIN & LUDY KLOSSKI

Before They Met

<u>Kevin</u> - Oak Hill, West Virginia, USA
Kevin was a Health and Safety Manager at a chemical plant in Houston, Texas for 10 years before he became disabled, requiring two hip replacement surgeries. "It was a very good job," Kevin said. "Then I came down with a disease called avascular necrosis in my hips and I could not climb the towers anymore.

"I moved back to West Virginia to be with my family. I had a good life. I was living by myself. I love to read. I love to play basketball. I had a lot on my hands."

<u>Ludy</u> - Marilag, Catanduanes, Philippines
Ludy moved away from home and her mother and father to get a job in Manila. "Ludy worked at Shell as a cashier, I think for seven years. She had been there for a long time," Kevin said.

Meeting on Christian Filipina

When the couple first met on Christian Filipina, Ludy asked Kevin, "Will you be my friend?" "I was like, wow!" Kevin exclaimed. "This lady is beautiful! This lady is so sweet and so caring and so thoughtful toward other people. These were the characteristics I have been looking for in someone. When I met Ludy, we started out as friends and from there it just blossomed and we just started falling in love with each other.

"We kept talking and talking and we started video chatting," said Kevin. "We are laughing and giggling and we can't just wait to talk to each other, and we are just both excited now, knowing that we get to meet again. We've got a great and wonderful time every time that we talk," Kevin said. "I felt her dedication and her love for me. I told her that 'I have deep feelings about you and I think I am falling in love with you,' and she responded, 'I think I am falling in love with you too.'"

Christian Filipina has Integrity

Kevin appreciates the integrity and diligence he found on Christian Filipina. "Well, as you know, there are scammers. I met a few of those before I got to talk to Ludy. There was one and we did not really have a connection. I know for sure that she was a scammer; she asked for money and you blocked her."

Ludy has some advice for other ladies on Christian Filipina. She said, "I talked to other guys and it did not work out with them, but Kevin kept on sending messages. Select what is best for you. You can feel it when you love someone. You feel it deep in your heart; you know. Find what is real, if you can feel it in your heart. It's what I have been looking for in my life. I am so happy and so blessed."

Meeting in Person the First Time

After nearly a year of courtship on Christina Filipina, Kevin visited Ludy in the Philippines. They spent about three weeks together and "had a great tie" to one another. "We got along really great; the communication was not perfect but we still found ways to understand each other," said Kevin. "It was a blast!"

"I think nervous; happy and nervous. When I hugged him I asked myself, 'this is true?' I can't explain my feeling; I asked God, 'this is true, God?' I cannot believe that it happened!" Ludy said excitedly. She goes on, "My parents are so glad at how Kevin is there for me. My parents cannot believe there is a guy willing to meet or to show how I am a princess."

"I know all her family members and they treat me just like I am one of them," said Kevin happily. The second time Kevin visited, "We got a get together with family and friends; there were 60-70 people there. We went down to the ocean; there is a place where you can rent an area to have a party, rent a karaoke machine and swim in the ocean. It was a great time of fellowship and fun together.

"I am glad that I got to know Ludy for a year before we got married. I got to know her really well," said Kevin. Ludy said that she "is ready to move on to the next chapter of her life."

Two Special Wedding Days!

"This time, she got to come home with me and we get to start making our family and start our future dreams together!" Ludy, who is 30 years old, had never been on an airplane, and Kevin was concerned about her traveling alone, so he went back to the Philippines and escorted her "home" to her new life.

They got married about a month later on June 28, 2014. It was "a simple wedding. The pastor is my friend for years and he did it for us," said Kevin. "We orchestrated things to make it special. She had three bridesmaids and a ring bearer. She has a beautiful dress. It was hard to find her a dress; she is 4'11"! But we found one that fit her perfectly and she was absolutely beautiful. My dad gave her away since her dad is not here. We have several family and friends, so the church was full. She felt blessed and happy about it. Then we are going to get married again in the Philippines; that is where the big wedding will be held. We are really excited to get married in front of her family."

With a smile in his voice, Kevin said, "When she put her on wedding dress the first time, she was so happy, she had tears in her eyes; it was like, 'I do not want to take it off!' I told her she needs to because it needs to be steam cleaned and she was like, 'Oh, I have to give it away again!'" Ludy's lucky, though; she gets to wear it a second time!

Kevin said, "I told her that I want to be totally dedicated to her and she said she wants a family and she talks about how she wants to take care of me for the rest of our lives. We both want to have a baby; I hope it is not too late for me, being age 46. But that is definitely the main plan. We are hoping for a girl and a boy, Stephanie and Luke. I just think that Stephanie is a beautiful name and she picked the name Luke." Ludy said, "Luke is kind of like a combination of Ludy and Kevin!"

"My mother loves Wilma a lot; her attitude, her kindness, her meekness, her humility. My mother took to her right away. Wilma was very open when meeting my family. She is very easy to get along with. She was looking to fit in."

3

BARAK & WILMA STASIOWSKI

Before They Met

Barak - Sessner, Florida, USA

"I had just moved to Florida after a rough 2008. I had a separation, a divorce, a bankruptcy, a job loss and a foreclosure. It was quite a year and the money was low," Barak remembered. "It made my decision fairly easy to come to Florida and live with family, and then I had more time because I was collecting unemployment insurance. I enjoyed my first six months of unemployment, relaxing." At 57, "I lost 30 pounds because I was concentrating on me for a change instead of on work.

"I had been married almost half my life and I enjoyed being married for a lot of good reasons," Barak said. "As I said in my profile, the 'Man-cation' had gone on long enough. It's a funny expression I came up with, meaning a single guy who doesn't have any ties, any worries, and sort of a single guy that's on vacation. It started to get boring and I started to miss the association of a good woman.

"I've been a truck driver for 14 years," and time is limited. "It's certainly hard to meet people because you're alone in the truck; you have your phone but you don't know who to call," Barak said.

<u>Wilma</u> - General Santos City, Philippines

Wilma, who is now 33, explained, "When I was young I needed to work hard to graduate high school. I had a simple life in the Philippines. I've got my mom and dad. I've got three sisters and one brother. I have many nieces and nephews. I worked from 13 years old until 29. I worked like planting in the ground; worked in Manila in a factory; worked as a sales lady; worked as a housemaid."

Give Her a Wink!

Wilma took her time looking for the right person. "I tried many other websites," she said. "I can say Christian Filipina is the best. I liked when gentleman gave you a wink, and then after giving a wink they're giving you a message, then they open a chat, so you can chat also. So for me Christian Filipina is a good opportunity to meet people looking for someone."

"I was just patiently looking at some of the websites," said Barak. "Christian Filipina was just very simple to use. I liked that the introductions were already completed for you. Really, you are looking for someone to meet and talk to and develop a relationship with, and so are they. Rather than chit-chat in the vegetable aisle, I chose to meet someone in a direct situation where I knew I was looking, and they were looking, and that part is already taken care of. You still have to be careful. Developing any relationship takes questions and answers. And if you like the answers then you ask another question, and you just keep on going with that; you're fine. If the answers start turning a different color from what you expected, then at some point the questions stop. So I found that to be true at Christian Filipina, that I might reach a point in a conversation that it wasn't working; then I would politely say, 'I'm sorry, but we don't seem to have compatibility,' and it was that much easier to end the relationship through Christian Filipina."

Getting to Know Each Other

"It only took about a month of conversation" before Barak knew that Wilma was the one. "We were talking at least 10 hours a week and we were on messages and camera and I just began to find out more and more about her. I'd say it was probably about the time where she was interested enough in changing her religious beliefs according to mine. I was ready to make a major change in my life by being committed to someone new, even though she was 10,000 miles away. I needed to see a strong commitment on Wilma's part in order for us to be a good match. I found out that she had already been researching my religion, Jehovah's Witnesses, and she had already developed some friendships among the Witnesses. So I knew she was serious and that we would be a good match.

"I hit that 7th week where my mind and my heart were fully involved. I was already telling her the 'L' word, you know, L-O-V-E?" he laughed. "I was falling in love with her. You think, 'how is that possible when they haven't met face-to-face?' It's possible! When you know what you want in life, it's very possible. Wilma is what I want."

Wilma added, "I chose him. He's a religious person. He's a Jehovah's Witness and I know a Jehovah's Witness is a good person. I think his profile showed a good personality. I think everything is going good."

Meeting in Person and Meeting Her Family

"We talked about so many things, so that when we met it really wasn't a big surprise," said Barak. "What was a big surprise was her body language; the way she held herself, the way she laughed and tilted her head back and the big smile. Of course, that was very attractive. We were totally honest with each other and told each other what we expected.

"I met just about all of her family and talked with them all somewhat. Their English was nowhere near her English, so it was difficult. So they just said 'yes' a lot, and if on camera, smiled a lot. But they conveyed warmth I could understand. I was welcomed by everything they said or did. They never felt like I was stealing Wilma away. They never felt threatened. They were happy that Wilma was happy."

Applying for a K-1 Fiancée Visa

"We got engaged the week that I went there, so I had known her only seven weeks! I told her, 'Well, Honey, I love you and I'm pretty sure you love me, and we're going to do the best we can to have a good life together. We'll do our best because I want to have a child with you,' and based on that she was willing to go through with the engagement and we've been married two years. The main thing is we're together and getting to know each other and very close in our bond.

"I brought her in on K-1 fiancée visa." The immigration process "was time consuming. I didn't want any mistakes. I wanted to make sure it was done right the first time, and it was, but there were still a couple of small hiccups with her National Bureau of Investigation report. She has a very common name and had to wait for five days to get her report cleared. Her medical report was in Manila, so she had to go and stay there. She called every day crying!"

The couple married March 16, 2012 at the Tower Hall in Tampa. They had a simple wedding where family and friends attended. "For the reception, we went to a beach restaurant," Wilma said. "I need to respect my husband and I love him, so I need to protect him. Barak and I, we're happy together!"

A Perfect Daughter-in-Law

Barak said, "My mother loves Wilma a lot; her attitude, her kindness, her meekness, her humility. My mother took to her right away. Wilma was very open when meeting my family. She is very easy to get along with. She was looking to fit in. She would go right into the kitchen of any of my family's houses and would offer to clean dishes or help cook the meal. My mom was 91 in June and she just loves Wilma to death, like her own daughter! Wilma does all of the things that a daughter-in-law should do, really: spend time with her mother-in-law, help her, do small things for her, and my mom just can't stop talking about Wilma. She doesn't know what she would do without Wilma."

"I'm a Happy Guy!"

Things are looking up for Barak and Wilma. "Presently I have my own business" transporting cars," Barak said, and he does a lot of driving. The couple is looking forward to making his local and long-haul runs together. "I like going around and seeing different places," said Wilma.

"I almost got in a bar fight last week! I was bragging. 'I'm happy! I'm a happy guy!' The other guys at the bar, they were truck drivers, and some were asking questions about meeting wonderful ladies online. But others were becoming upset because they felt that a lot of these websites are not real, are not true, and are not helping people find people."* But Barak replied to them, "the separation of who was the best match was easy on Christian Filipina, just the simplicity of it; no one was putting on a show. With Christian Filipina, what you see is what you get!"

*Based on our research, Christian Filipina found this to be true. Most international dating sites are fraudulent. Christian Filipina is one of the few legitimate services.

4

FOREST & GRACE ROSWELL

Before They Met

Forest - Central Point, Oregon, USA

"I was in a depression and lonely," Forest said. "I had just gone through a divorce about two or three years before." Forest was married for 38 years and had two boys. "I was a truck driver just before I retired at 62. I worked for a company that hauls mail for the post office. It was short haul; about 150 miles, one way, at night. It's like being your own boss. You get a little tired at times and you have to stay focused 100%, all the time. For me it was a little difficult to meet people. I am not a real social person, so I pretty much stayed by myself."

Grace - Talisay, Negros Occidental, Philippines

"I became widowed 10 years ago but never opened myself to a relationship for quite long until my cousin suggested I join Christian Filipina," said Grace. "I worked hard to send my children to school until they finished. Now that they are on their own, it's time to give me the last episode and find the real man of my heart, care for him, and be with him for the rest of my life; a Christ-centered relationship that would last for a lifetime. I hoped and prayed and found one here. I am a one-man woman and not a materialistic one."

Looking for the "Last Episode" on Christian Filipina

"At one point, I was a little disappointed" about women, Forest said. "I did a little bit of dating after my divorce and I hadn't found them to be very honest. Everybody puts on a false front and then you find out what they are really like after a couple of months." Forest tried other dating sites first. "I met a few women, but most of them were not totally honest with what they were telling me about themselves.

"I had always been curious about Filipinas; I heard about them," said Forest. "Then I found this Christian Filipina site. It is set up in such a way that it worked for me. You can see the description, what they were writing about themselves. I was very happy that I was able to get in touch with someone who I wanted to spend the rest of my life with!

"When I first used it, I was getting a big head because I was getting letters from all ages of women!" said Forest sheepishly. "I knew what I wanted, even though it boosted my ego a little bit. All these women wanted to talk to me but I knew I wanted somebody that made me happy in the long run. I wanted somebody who was attuned to something that I wanted and not much different from my age. I finally found Grace" who is 59 and she "was the one that the most closely matched what I wanted in a wife and she is the one I chose."

Grace was on another site first, too "Some of the other websites are not honest; some people are just playing games. Some of the men are kind, but some not. Men on other websites especially have more vices, so you cannot find that they are good. That is why I chose a Seventh- day Adventist man. But Christian Filipina is honest, and is good, and the other members of the site are Godly and Christian. I heard that there are many Filipina women who married from Christian Filipina."

"It was hard," admitted Forest. "Because we know how much we love each other." Long distance relationships "take patience, but it helped us to develop an even closer relationship. We were able to get online and talk to each other on Facebook pretty much every day. We were keeping in touch, at least.

"Just like Grace, Filipinas are very family-oriented and faithful. They are very devoted to family," Forest said. "We were both praying about our relationship. About four months into our talking back and forth, I asked her to be engaged and she said 'Yes!'"

"I found a husband at Christian Filipina. We just got married; I am happily married." Grace added simply, "I fell in love with this guy!"

Traveling to the Philippines

"If you are a truck driver, you have access to computers," Forest said. "Christian Filipina is probably one of the best sites. I mean, if truckers have an interest to meet a good wife, a Christian, they can take a trip over there and meet somebody. I think they have three weeks for the visit, but that can be extended if they want to get an idea of what it feels like. If they like her, then they can apply for a fiancée visa and then go from there."

Forest took two trips to the Philippines. "The first trip, I got married and I stayed over there for about six months. Basically I was terrified! I had never met her and we were getting married the next day. I was questioning what I got myself into! The first night we did a lot of talking.

"Then I made another trip over there because I thought her visa would be issued," said Forest. The visa wasn't issued, however, and they had to wait so long that Forest went home to the United States for a while.

Two Weddings!

"We were married a day after I got to the Philippines," said Forest. "It was beautiful! We got married in a hotel and had a reception and everything there. It was great. My wife is a seamstress and she made her own dress, plus all the bridesmaid's dresses. She did a fantastic job!"

Grace remembers that it was a lot of work to make all the dresses so quickly. "I did not expect Forest would come in July. That is why I did not buy the cloth yet. I made three bridesmaids dresses, one maid of honor and three flower girls all in one week. I only eat for two hours and I work for 24 hours!"

"Actually, we got married two different times," Forest said. "We got married in the hotel; then when we got back to her cousin's city, the mayor married us again. I guess it was the tradition of the local area that you need to be married by the local mayor."

"We got married July 29, 2012 with a pastor. It was a ceremony wedding in our church." Grace explained, "Then we got married again with the mayor on August 25. I am so excited! I love this guy very much. All my sisters, my brothers, cousins, all were there. We had only invited 60 people. Close friends, my family, my daughter and my sons attended my wedding. I am so very happy that I married again."

Getting to Know the Family

After the wedding, "We stayed with her cousin for a month," said Forest. "We did a little sightseeing. Then we went back to her island where her house is to get better acquainted with her kids. Then we took a couple of trips to some resorts, which was like a honeymoon."

Forest said, "Everybody welcomed me with open arms! We went to a resort up in the mountains and rented a cabin and I think probably three or four kids showed up and we lived there, all sleeping in one big room. Not a lot of privacy, but we enjoyed it. There were a lot of activities in the resort that bonded us as a family." Grace added, "They like Forest; he is so very kind. He is an understanding and loving husband."

Immigration Was Tough

Forest has a little advice for other Christian Filipina couples. "If you do not want to wait a long time like we did, it is much better to apply for a fiancée visa, instead of getting married over there. It was almost two years before she got her visa. My son also married a Filipina. He was over there visiting me and found somebody and they are about ready to come over to the United

States and get married."

It took so long that, "We talked about living in the Philippines quite a bit because she had a house there, but it was hot; too humid for me. My first six months there, I lost 65 pounds!" said Forest. Grace added, "I am proud of him. He stayed there for more than six months. My friends and family are so happy that I have a husband like Forest!"

Smiling Every Day!

"Now she is trying to make an adjustment here, since it is cooler for her" in Oregon, Forest laughed. "Philippines and Oregon are a big difference!" added Grace.

"I love him because he is very good and so very kind. In conversation, he is very patient; sometimes I get disconnected while speaking and he is still there listening," Grace said gratefully. "I am happy. His family and his kids, I like them also. I like his place because it is in the countryside. He has a farm here."

"She takes care of me and I take care of her," Forest said. "We found a few Filipina ladies that she can be friends with and talk to, and everything is positive for our future. I wake up with a smile every day!"

"She takes care of me and I take care of her. We found a few Filipina ladies that she can be friends with and talk to, and everything is positive for our future. I wake up with a smile every day."

"It's like we're both lucky and we won a lotto, because it's like I am so beautiful and a special girl for him as his fiancée. I have a blessing from Lord now, and I like serving God with my beloved husband until the Lord comes."

24

5

GEERT & JENNEFFER STEELANDT

Before They Met

Geert - Menen, Belgium

"I am a born again Christian for three years now. I am baptized and going to church every Sunday," Geert said. At 43, he decided that he wanted "a serious relationship that leads to marriage. I had been a very long time looking for a woman," so decided to look "for a born-again Christian lady who is sweet, kind, loving and loves Jesus more than anything else." He found his life partner in Jenneffer.

Jenneffer - Calbiga, Western Samar, Philippines

"I am simple woman from a simple family and am the youngest of eight children," Jenneffer said. "I love reading, dancing sometimes, and cooking. I am an independent person in terms of living, and work as an independent distributor of World Class Wellness products" in the Philippines while she waits for her visa and her move to Belgium to be with husband Geert.

"I am a born-again Christian at the Main Street Christian Fellowship Full Gospel Church," said Jenneffer. "I love doing my ministries, sharing and fellowship." She has a message for Christian Filipina ladies: "I advise members who have a desire to have a Godly man to pray for what you really want in your life and always seek God's presence. God answers our prayers all the time in his perfect time. Do your part and God will do the rest. Ask, believe and claim it all the way!"

Looking for Your New Life on Christian Filipina

A friend of Geert's married a Filipina and recommended Geert do the same. "I registered with the Christian Filipina site to meet my new life," Geert said. He agreed with his friend, "Filipina women are easier and more open than Belgian women and faithful to their husbands." He remained a member "until I met my wife Jenneffer. I'm very thankful to the Lord for answering my prayer and thankful also to this site which God used as a channel of blessings for me and other people."

Jenneffer has tried other sites before and didn't like them "because most of them are not totally serious and they are not Christian members," she said. At 30 years old, Jenneffer knows what she wants. "It's been good chatting with members of the site who are God's children because you share your faith and God's name will be glorified. I like Christian Filipina very much because more members here are most genuinely Christian."

Going to the Philippines

Geert has been to the Philippines four times, the first trip in 2010 was to see a friend. Back then he was a "little bit scared, but when I saw that people are friendly, then I became relaxed and found out I like Filipina girls! Then when I met Jenneffer on the Christian Filipina site, I decided to go to the Philippines again. I learned that people in the Philippines believe more in Jesus than people in Belgium and I learned also that their faith is genuine and true. I learned also about the food and culture."

Getting to Know Each Other

"I remember the first time we met," mused Jenneffer. "Pastor Sonny made a blind date for both of us. He is the one who met Geert upon his arrival at the Aquino Airport and our witness for our courtship. Pastor Sonny is the Pastor of a Full Gospel Church in Taguig."

Pastor Sonny sent a text message to Jenneffer, requesting to meet her at a restaurant in Pasig City, Manila on her way back from a church retreat in Tagatay. Jenneffer recalled the night vividly: "Pastor Sonny never said anything about Geert. When I was in the door of McDonalds, there was a man who shook hands with me and had a camera and making a video. He said, 'I'm Pastor Sonny, and Geert is with me now at the table.' I saw his back and I'm nervous and I don't really expect that Geert was there. And I felt like a superstar or celebrity because of the video recording and I felt conscious about what I'm saying because of the camera and people in McDonalds all seeing me. And I shook Geert's hand and say 'I'm Jenn' and he said 'I am Geert, how are you?'

"I'm nervous and I don't understand what I feel during that time," said Jenneffer. "I'm so blushed because I never expect I see my friend, so I excuse myself and I go to the comfort room. I make myself good, I do my hair and then go back to the table, and I see a flower and chocolate beside him. I admired him. 'Wow, who am I?' I say to myself."

Pastor Sonny went to another table and he gave us time to spend for knowing each other. I am so proud during that time because I'm so loved of the Lord because he give me a gift and he knew that I felt good and happy." Jenneffer said, "We eat together and got to know each other and he said to me, 'Jenn I like you!' and he gave his flower to me and he gave also the chocolate, and I felt so very special during that time. Ohhh, very much happy! I said only to him, 'Thank you Geert!' And now we are both happy, by God's grace."

Accepting Geert's Proposal

"Geert respects me a great deal and this is the reason why I fell in love with him," said Jenneffer. This love comes from God because Geert's spirit and my spirit are one. In the midst of every topic and situation that we have, we felt the presence of God and his full guidance. And the reason why I accepted Geert's proposal to become his fiancée is the word 'your body is a temple and my body is a temple.' Our bodies are temples of God and we don't do things that are against the law of God in terms of love. That very day, God answered my prayer that the man in front of me is the man God will prepare for me, and I answer Geert, 'Yes!' God is so good because we both experienced his faithfulness and protection from temptation."

Church Every Sunday

Seven months later, Geert went again to visit Jenneffer, who told us she "picked up him at the airport and he met my parents in Quezon City. In his 21 days stayed here he spent his time with me. He knows my family status, my siblings, my parents, and he accepts my family.

"We got together every Sunday and went to church while he was in the Philippines and we had dinner with my sister in the church," said Jenneffer. "We enjoyed our 21 days. We planned to go to Boracay Island to celebrate God's answering our prayers, but still we heard God's voice from there. We both cried because we cannot believe how God is so great in our lives. We both want simple lives and are a simple man and woman. We met in our life because we are both looking for a born-again Christian mate."

A Beautiful Garden Wedding!

"We got married March 30, 2014. The wedding day was at U.P. Diliman University Hotel in Quezon City, Manila. We were together with our closest friends and relatives, and the ceremony was officiated by Pastor Richard Bernardino, our senior Pastor." Jenneffer said, "This is the day that the Lord has made for both of us. God answered our prayer in his perfect time."

Blessings from the Lord

"It's like we're both lucky and we won a lotto, because it's like I am so beautiful and a special girl for him as his fiancée!" Jenneffer said excitedly. "But in spiritual matters, what I have right now is God's grace for me and him because we are not perfect. But we felt that we are perfect because it's God design for both of us to explore our life with each other in God's timing. What I have now is a blessing from the Lord, and I like serving God with my beloved husband until the Lord comes."

"I want to thank this godly website for ministering to us singles! Christian Filipina changed my life. So I thank you so much from the bottom of my heart. God bless you and God bless your ministry there at Christian Filipina."

6

JIMMY & JENNY KEALEY

Before They Met

Jimmy - Oak Lawn, Illinois, USA

"I am a 1st grade teacher," Jimmy told us. "I just turned 51 but I am very physically active and I have been told by many people that I look like I am in my mid-thirties. I love staying healthy and fit. I exercise four to five times a week for my spouse, myself and the Lord, who dwells within me.

"I am a man walking with the Lord. My faith is really strong. Jesus is #1 in my life! I try to glorify him each day and become more like him in words and deeds. I regularly attend church, read my Bible every day, pray often, spend quality time with the Lord, and believe that we are called by the Lord to share God's good news whenever the Spirit leads us. To me, Christianity is a personal relationship with Jesus, not a religion!"

Jenny - Manila, Philippines

"I'm a teacher here" in the Philippines and have two brothers, Jenny tells us. "I'm turning 26 years old. I'm easy to get along with. I am friendly, but sometimes at first, a bit shy. Also, I am a serious person, yet funny. I like singing and listening to Christian gospel songs.

"Accept the love Jesus has for you and be the best for the Lord," Jenny said.

There is no Better Website than ChristianFilipina.com!

Jimmy started looking for a lady four years ago. "I tried to start with the most popular Christian sites but some of them really did not have much as far as traffic or volume. The one that really advertises did not seem to connect me with anyone that was a good match with me, and so I found Christian Filipina and then I started meeting some quality women.

"The main thing I looked for was a godly born-again woman who is intelligent and really lives a good life and cares for her family. I have nothing but good things to say about Filipina women," Jimmy said. "They are genuine, and they are loyal, and they are submissive in a godly way. They are really gentle, wonderful women. Everyone I have corresponded with on your website, they were genuine. I never found any deception or lies or anything with any of them. I am so blessed that I have met them and I still pray for those who are still single. Your website, I can say that it is the best website out there for Christians! Especially for someone who wants to meet a godly Filipina woman. There is no better website! I've been on five or six of them, but none can be compared to yours for the genuine godliness of the women. Men are going to find themselves a queen in the Philippines.

"I want to thank this godly website for ministering to us singles! Christian Filipina changed my life. So I thank you so much from the bottom of my heart," said Jimmy gratefully. "God bless you and God bless your ministry there at Christian Filipina. I think you are going to see, when you get to heaven, how many lives you have touched with your ministry. It is a great website, and if I have more Christian friends and they are looking for a good wife, I will definitely recommend your site and tell them that I only met and got to really know women personally when I spent a few dollars and subscribed here for a while, so if you can afford even the lowest membership rate for a while, God may bless you like he did me."

"I joined here because I am looking for a lifetime partner who is Christian too, with same belief as I, that Jesus is our Lord and Savior," said Jenny. "Thank you ChristianFilipina.com. May God bless you always! You did a good job. Continue serving other people and the Lord. More power!

"May God bless you with your search for the love of your life. Be a man of God first before being a man of a woman's heart," Jenny advised. "Seek God first before finding a partner and surely the love you are waiting for will be given to you, unconditionally. God has the perfect plan for you; you deserve the best. My testimony may help you to find a real Christian woman. I pray for that woman. I pray for both of you if you already found her. Take care and have a blessed day."

Eager to Meet in Person

Jimmy spent about a year on ChristianFilipina.com before he met Jenny. "And I met my lovely wife in June of 2012, and I decided that I didn't want to spend two to three months conversing over the internet before I go and meet someone if I am serious about them, so I went and met her in July."

"There's a big gap in age, so I asked her, 'Why would you consider marrying someone my age? Could it be a problem?'" confided Jimmy. "And she said, 'Usually that would be, but I can tell that you are physically active and you look young and you are really into exercise and fitness, so it should not be a problem.' So we got over that hurdle pretty quickly."

"My strategy was to visit several women, but Jenny was number one on my list," said Jimmy. "She was the one I felt the most compatible with, but I was supposed to visit four when I was there because I had been there a year before from a different website and I only visited one and it did not work out. So I thought this time I would visit several and see which one the Lord has for me based on the chemistry, and compatibility and how she felt about me."

Jimmy spent three weeks in the Philippines. "That was pretty much what I could afford then. I am a school teacher, so summer I have off. It worked out well. I spent the first week with Jenny and I went to visit one other woman on another island. I visited two others and had fellowship with them, but after those three other visits, I felt that Jenny was the one for me.

"We were both attracted and had chemistry over the internet, but that does not always translate to good chemistry in person. So we wanted to make sure that it was really a good connection," Jimmy said. "Jenny was not too happy about me going to meet the other ones, but when I came back, she told me she was jealous in a good way. I told her that I needed to confirm that she was the one for me. After I came back, I had no doubts that she was the only one for me. So it kinda' reinforced what I thought and it drew her closer to me. Having me interested, possibly, in someone else made her realize how much she loved me."

Passing "The Mom Test"

"The protectiveness of her mother was a little bit of a surprise, but your website informed me how close Filipino families are. It did not surprise me that the family would be very involved with our visit. So the first time I met her she told me that she wanted her mom to be with her, and being a grown woman it kinda' took me back a little bit, but then I realized the cultural aspect of it and I thought that was fine. I thought I needed to know her mom, as well. They have a close-knit family unit and I passed 'The Mom Test' on the first visit! I think it went pretty well. Then after that she was a little more open and at ease in meeting me one-on-one in a public setting. So I was a little surprised, but not shocked, that her mom was with her during the first visit."

Things, "actually progressed pretty quickly," Jimmy said. "We just started meeting a couple of times after her work and we grew closer and closer and I felt connected to her. There was no language barrier and she is of the same faith as me. We're both pretty strong Christians. That was the common bond that united us, but there was also chemistry and we both found each other attractive. We had a lot to talk about, being both teachers, so that connected us even further and from there it just kinda' took off, and then within a few days of me returning, we were falling in love."

Anxious to be Married!

"Three to four days after that I proposed to her and she accepted, and then we started making arrangements and figure out when we would get married. I proposed to her, but I had to go through the process of asking for her hand in marriage with her parents," said Jimmy. "They drilled me pretty good on why I wanted to marry their daughter. I told them, 'Look at your daughter: she is pretty, she is godly, she is smart, she is very pleasant. Why wouldn't I marry your daughter?' Then they asked her, 'Are you sure this is the guy?' and she said 'Yes.' They allowed me to move forward with the relationship. I wanted to give her an engagement ring and we ended up doing that the night before I left.

"I really wanted to get married right away, being a little over-anxious in hindsight," said Jimmy, "but she said 'We need to take it slower than that, maybe three to four months.' So we just said 'You know, we are gonna' keep in touch and we are going to write each other letters and we'll do instant messaging and all that."

Jimmy came back again for 10 days in October. "We even grew closer during that time; we set the date for the marriage in December," said Jimmy.

"Please pray for us. I am now happily married to my husband, Jimmy. I am so blessed!" Jenny said excitedly. "I thank the Lord for giving me the love of my life. I can't ask for more. He is the one I was praying for. The Lord really gives the desires of your heart if you will be faithful to him. God is so good, all the time! Amen!"

Is She the Sole Breadwinner Back Home?

"I think if someone is from another country and they want to bring a Filipina woman back into their country, they would like to take into consideration the financial aspect, because a lot of the women in the Philippines may come from low income families and they may be the sole breadwinner for the family, which my wife is," Jimmy said thoughtfully. "So we may have to provide support for them, which I don't have a problem doing. I want the gentlemen to consider the fact that you are marrying into their family and they are so loyal to their family, which is a really good quality, and that they are going to say, 'How is my family going to be provided for?' and that is a legitimate concern. I understand that. 'Am I willing to send $500 a month, or whatever, to my wife's family because she was the main breadwinner and now I am taking her away from her family?' That is something that men need to consider, but it shouldn't really be the main thing.

"That is something I would strongly recommend to discuss in detail before they set the wedding date, because if they cannot come to a realistic number for both of them, then they are going to have money arguments," advised Jimmy. "We did discuss it, and we came up with a number and I followed through. Her mom passed away, and there were burial and funeral charges, the cemetery lot and things like that."

Jimmy said Jenny is "actually starting up an internet cafe business in her neighborhood, so there are some other unexpected expenses, but nothing that is going to break my bank. That is something that they might consider too, like; 'How can we start a business for your family to support them when you're gone?' And the woman could get that started before she goes to another country. That is what my wife is doing right now; she is starting an internet cafe business and she is going to pass it on to her brothers, who will administer the business when she is gone."

"If they want to stay in the Philippines and live there, and they like the weather and they like the environment, it is probably a lot cheaper than in the United States or any of the more developed countries," Jimmy said truthfully.

The Future Will Fall Into Place

Filipina women "are hard workers," said Jimmy appreciatively. "And she wants to work while here, and I told her we'd like to have a couple of kids first and I don't really want her working while our kids are being raised until about the age of five or six because those are the crucial developmental years. I want to have a God-honoring family with two or three children. I love kids!

"The main thing is we are both strong believers in Jesus. Stay close to Jesus: 'And my God will meet all your needs according to his glorious riches in Christ Jesus.' Philippians 4:19. I guess after that I think God will just let everything fall into place," Jimmy said.

Jenny concluded, "Remember, God already has plans for you from the very start; from when you were born until today. Jeremiah 1:5:"Before I shaped you in the womb, I knew all about you. Before you saw the light of day, I had holy plans for you ... "

7

KERMIT & RAQUEL GEESAMAN

Before They Met

Kermit - Tennville, Indiana &Aubury, Texas, USA

"I have been divorced for almost five years," Kermit said sadly. "I have been married twice before; the first time for 12 years and the second time for 15 years. So I have been pourin' out everything that I had: my heart and my life. Between the two marriages, I have 15 children and 32 grandchildren! Nine are my blood and the other six I raised from my second marriage."

Kermit has driven a truck for 35 years. "I drive for a small company. They have 12 trucks.I do a lot of long haul, and once in a while, short local. Our lives are really confined behind the wheel and we have the 10-hour break." Kermit even conducted his interview on the road, "I am in Ohio right now, on my way to Pennsylvania today and then I will be in Indiana."

Kermit sure is a busy guy, so busy, in fact, that he keeps two residences! "I live in Indiana and Texas and am between both places all the time. I pay taxes in Indiana because that is where my job is based. I work in between Tennville in Indiana and Aubury, a little town in Texas, North of Dallas-Fort Worth."

It can be difficult for truckers to meet people. "It is probably a good thing to focus on truck drivers, because they are out here on the road. A lot of truckers now carry laptops. I see that a lot now," Kermit observed. ChristianFilipina.com "is a good opportunity for someone out here on the road. There are a lot of good guys and there are a lot of good aspects to truckers. Americans I have seen with Filipinas always raise my curiosity. I am a people watcher. I have always been, so I watch them and I watch how the lady treats them and I have seen gold.

"I am also a minister and I love to do missionary work," said Kermit. "I am kind of an evangelist; it is what I do now. I am Protestant. My license is non-denominational so that I can go to any Baptist or Methodist or Pentecostal church and be able to preach."

Raquel - Naawan, Misamis Oriental, Philippines
"I am 27 years old and I am still at home taking care of my mother. And also, my dad is a pastor and I help him in the church. I've been a vice president of the church before. Sometimes, I teach on church missions and I do Bible study every Sunday. I talk to many people."

Wanting to Marry a Filipina

Kermit had been married more than half his life and at 52 decided he wanted to marry again. "I wanted somebody in my life; it felt like it was long enough. I stayed single for almost five years; then I began to think about a Filipina wife. I had seen a few Filipina ladies in the United States and I have noticed the way they treat their husbands and the way they take care of them. I have some friends, one with a Filipina wife and the other one married a Colombian. I noticed how both ladies take care of their husbands and I really wanted that. I wanted someone that was God-fearing first, someone that would be loving and faithful. I felt like I could see that through a Filipina lady.

"I was very skeptical about the web," Kermit admitted. "I had my doubts about whether that would work or not for me. So I begin to pray about it. I started looking through a couple of different sites and it was so complicated; it was hard to complete the information. Then I went to Christian Filipina; the only thing I have as far as a computer is a smart phone. When the Christian Filipina site came up it was very easy.

"I thought that I need to write personally and I was able to pour my heart out in the profile but was still skeptical of the whole situation. Not really knowing if this is what I was supposed to do, not knowing if this is what I wanted to do, because I kept thinking that I am just going to be single because I do not want to get hurt again. I was protecting myself."

So Many Ladies to Choose From on ChristianFilipina.com

"I called a friend, the one with a Filipina wife, and talked to him about it and I said 'Okay.' It was a half hour later one of the ladies from Christian Filipina called me up," said Kermit. "I talked to her and said 'Maybe I will try this.' I signed up on the Platinum side. Then all the matches came up, I thought, 'This is crazy. There is no way that I am going to spend this much time looking through all these ladies.' Then I looked at Raquel's picture and I looked in her eyes and that was it!

"I deleted everybody else. I did not talk to them; I do not believe in that. Some of the guys said to me, 'Maybe you need to pick three; then choose from there and go see them,' and I said, 'Nope; if I go to the Philippines, I am going for one lady,'" Kermit said. "I believe that if you put in your profile truly and as a real person to the best of your knowledge, you are going to receive a real person, a real lady that will stand by you for the rest of your life. So, when I saw Raquel's picture, there was nothing else that mattered. It was not about her beauty. When I looked in her eyes I could see something that sparked what I desired. That's what everyone should look for and pray for. Choose one lady and choose her and only her. I did, and I met the love of my life!

"It was not long after I met Raquel that I knew without a doubt," said Kermit. "When I told her that I was a pastor and she told me that her dad was a minister, and then I absolutely knew! There was no doubt in my mind that I had made the right choice."

Raquel said, "I chose Kermit because he is a good guy and he is serious. And also, he has strong faith in God just like me. That is why I adore him. He is funny also, just like me! I'm so thankful to God for blessing me with a God-fearing man and Christian and for loving me truly. I couldn't ask for more."

Many Thanks for ChristianFilipina.com!

"Christian Filipina helped me very much," Raquel said. "It is an awesome site. I think Christian Filipina let me find my love, my partner, my husband in life. I like Christian Filipina because I met Kermit there. I am so much in love with my husband. I am so happy and I hope that God will bring more marriages because Filipinas are dreaming to have a partner in life. And to those still single out there, just keep praying and asking for God's guidance because when God promises it is always, 'Yes!' Just wait for his perfect timing!"

"Thanks, Christian Filipina, for everything. You are a wonderful agency!" Kermit said excitedly. "May God bless all your staff. We both are so thankful for you guys, for your site. It was a tool that God used for us to be together. Thank you so much Lord Jesus Christ. Amen."

Different Lifestyles, Different Traditions, Different Problems

"Because I did some study, I knew a little bit about the Filipino culture and I knew about the circumstances in which they live. Their lives are different from ours: different lifestyles, different family traditions. You cannot be a spoiled person and go there," warned Kermit. "Some guys have problems with it, but if you want a Filipina lady, you need to do your study on different traditions and be prepared to set down outside or on the dirt floor inside the house and eat whatever they eat. Make sure to pray over the food.

"I felt like I had a promise from God," Kermit confided. "I knew that he was going to take care of me; I really did not fear" to travel to the Philippines. "I heard the horror stories, but being a truck driver, you're downtown in big cities; you already have the street knowledge and are prepared. You see people living under bridges. You see all kinds of things and so those things prepare you. God has prepared me all my life for this trip."

Kermit planned well. "I tried to work extra hours and tried to have things paid before I went. My wife went up and had my room paid. Part of our wedding was already paid. Everything for the flight was paid. Then I tried to set back money for my bills so I could pay them while I was gone. I found out that the flight was like $3,500; it was unreal. Then I stretched the trip out for a few more days to 28 days and it went down to $1,400.

"I went to my phone company first and asked if my phone will work when I get there, they said, 'Yes.' I got to Manila, I looked at my phone and it did not work," said Kermit. "I went to the ATM machine; it did not work. I had $56 in my pocket and I had to be in Manila for two days."

Kermit continued, "When I got there, it was 2:00 in the morning and the airport was absolutely packed. I walked around like a fish out of water, not knowing what to do. I stood over the crowd, above these people. I prayed to God, 'You will have to give me somebody that can direct me and get me to the embassy by morning.' I went where all the cabbies were, and one asked me if I need any help, if I needed to go somewhere. I said, 'I tell you what: my phone don't work, my bank card don't work and I do not know how I can go to the U.S. Embassy in the morning. He said he would get me a motel. I said, 'You don't understand; I cannot pay for a motel; my card is not working.' He said, 'Come on, get in.' He put me downtown, right across from the embassy; he took me inside, he said, 'Get this guy a room!' They tried my card and it worked in the motel!" The next morning, "I only have $40 in pesos. The cab took me back to their airport at noon and the plane did not leave until 8:00 a.m. the next day. I slept on the floor. I would do it all over again to have Raquel in my life. It was all worth it, everything I went through, and everything that happened to me, because she is worth it!

"Because we had spent so much time on the phone and on Skype and on the Christian Filipina site, texting back and forth and talking, I felt like I had already known her all my life. Then to meet her was so breathtaking. There she was! I was holding her in my arms. Then to be able to meet the whole family, they all came to the airport, and to meet them was just absolutely awesome. I have never felt so much outpouring of love and welcome-ness. You can tell through our pictures; you will see that they have made a great big banner and put it at the side of the house that says, 'Welcome to the Philippines, my love Kermit.' We stayed at her mom and dad's the whole day. They had a big welcome dinner for me there. It was awesome!" Kermit was emotional, "I never had anything like that before."

Raquel gave us her impressions: "When I saw him, he was so approachable and he always makes me smile and he is funny, really. He has humility and he can understand my family. When I met him, I felt that I knew him. Even though I knew him only for a short month; it's like I knew him for a year. Do you understand?"

"While I was over there, I had time to do two missions," Kermit said. "I went over to preach at the churches where her dad is also a pastor. They made me the missionary in 10 churches. Once we get her citizenship, we will be travelling back and forth, but we will live in the U.S."

The Feeling of Love was Astounding

Kermit and Raquel were married April 26, 2014. Kermit remembered fondly, "The wedding was at Rosewood Park, Naawan. We were very, very excited! It was a wonderful time, a wonderful experience; more than I can ask for. It was a good, traditional, family-oriented wedding. We had sponsors there, 20 men and 20 women. Even the Mayor was there and the City Council people. There was quite a crowd, probably 250 people, I would say. It seemed to me that the town showed up to bon voyage the wedding and to show their appreciation."

Kermit laughed, "When she got ready to put the ring on my finger, she grabbed my right hand and they started laughing. Raquel, she was crying. Most of the ladies there were wiping tears away and I was astonished at how much it meant to them and how much I meant to them. It was hard because I never felt that with my family.

"We had pig roast and then all the family members were there. The love that I felt from all of her family was just astounding," Kermit said sweetly. "To be able to look out across the crowd and see the many people and see that they were sincere, I have never felt that in my life.

The Future Can't Come Fast Enough

Kermit spoke of a photograph Raquel sent him before they were married. "I remember that picture. I told her, 'You know, the first time I saw you and saw the background of coconut trees in the jungle, I imagined myself there with you.' Now we have a picture together, standing, holding her, with that same background.

"When I see those pictures, every time I look in her eye, it is absolutely unexplainable." Kermit just wants Raquel to come "home." "I would like to get back over probably in another couple of months while waiting for her visa to come to the United States."

So does Raquel. "I am excited to go there to live with him and know we will get along. We have plans and go on with our life."

"We really have not decided yet where we will live," said Kermit. "I'd rather stay full time in the warmer climate. I am sure she will appreciate that because in Indiana it snows." Raquel agreed, "I think I want to go to Texas. I think in Texas it is like Philippines, because it is warm there."

In any event, Kermit's boss will let Raquel accompany him on his runs once she arrives. Kermit lets us in on his plans: "We will be going back and forth. We are going to travel the country for the first couple of years, maybe," said Kermit. Raquel's up for it: "I'd like to travel with him."

"At the same time I am driving, I am putting out my résumé to be a pastor. That is my main goal, to be a pastor and settle down and to get out of this truck!" said Kermit. "I want to be able to settle down before two years and to be a full time-minister in a designated church. In what town and what city, it is really up to God. I am praying faithfully, hoping that it is somewhere warm but I know God is working in that direction. My dad was a pastor for 44 years and I know that it is my ultimate calling, and my wife is 100% behind me. She does preach once in a while for her dad. She also has a gift and a calling on her life, as well. God brought us together to work together as a team for the ministry."

"And we will spread the word of God over there in the U.S.A.," added Raquel.

Christian Filipina asked them both if they want to have babies. "Yes! I am excited about it. I have only one name left in my pocket." It came to Kermit three years ago. "I said, 'Are you serious?' But I put it in my pocket, in my billfold, and that will be the name of our child, one of them, I guess. I want to spend a couple of years with her and our cultures and our different ways of life and get settled in. We will travel the States, and that, I am so excited about." About the babies, Raquel only said shyly, "In time."

"Thank you guys; thank you Christian Filipina so very, very much!" Kermit exclaimed. Thank you, Peter, for listening to the Word of God and starting this website. What I like about it is, if God used it as a tool, as a conduit, he directed me to Raquel, to my wife. If it had not been for Christian Filipina, I would not have met my bride. I will continue to keep you guys in prayer. I will recommend you to whoever I see that has a sincere heart. My heart goes out to those ladies. I pray that they also use the Christian Filipina site and I pray that the men are very truthful, not only to the lady that they talk to, but with themselves."

Kermit concluded, "I have found the beautiful bride that I will spend the rest of my life with."

"I think Christian Filipina let me find my love, my partner, my husband in life. I like Christian Filipina because I met Kermit there. I am so much in love with my husband. I am so happy and I hope that God will bring more marriages."

"For those who are really hoping to find the perfect match, just wait and wait and have patience and ask, or pray very, very hard; patience and prayer. There is really someone for them, a soulmate for them. In time, God's perfect time, he or she will meet them for eternity."

8

ALEX & DESIREE LABA

Before They Met

<u>Alex</u> - Toronto, Ontario, Canada

"My name is Alex. I am 31 years old. I grew up in Chernovtsy, a small city in Western Ukraine, but also spent many years living in the country, which I love much better than living in the big city. I've lived in Toronto since 1998. I came here when I was 15. My parents came here for better life. I am old-school, family oriented. I have wonderful parents, who are my best friends and my mentors. The most influential people in my life are my grandparents, and my grandmother was the one who brought me up since my toddler years. I owe them my life," Alex said earnestly.

"I work as a logistics lead at Sears." Alex explained,

"Logistics is shipping, receiving merchandise in the store and providing customer service.

"I love cooking Eastern European food and learning different cuisines, traveling and anything to do with nature and outdoors," said Alex. "I'm also a major movie and music collector."

<u>Desiree</u> - San Fernando, Pampanga, Philippines
"I'm an easy going person, down to earth, honest, lovable, caring, sincere, sweet, thoughtful, spontaneous and a one-man woman," Desiree said.

At 29, Desiree has a nice career: "I currently work as a public school teacher here in Angeles City, Pampanga. I finished my Bachelor of Elementary Education at Holy Angel University. I have two siblings; they are also teachers. We came from a family of teachers."

ChristianFilipina.com Crafts A Love Story!

Alex had been on two other sites, one "website went as far as stating the kind of professions; women were looking for how much money a man made. As far as the conversation, it never went farther than that first meeting online. I went physically on one date but I didn't feel any chemistry."

Desiree agreed, "I joined other sites before, but unfortunately, I did not have the success to meet a serious guy that would really commit himself to settling down into marriage. I joined the Christian Filipina site three years ago. I was encouraged by my sister, who unfortunately passed away two years ago; so she was the one who really encouraged me to join the Christian Filipina site. I have encountered several guys there but it was not actually to the point that we took it to a serious relationship," until she met Alex, her leading man.

"My best friend at work is Filipino," said Alex. "He introduced me to the culture, to values, to morals; to Filipino people in general. He was the one that was looking for me for a girl because he knew I was having a hard time finding a woman in general. Christian Filipina came to me out of the blue; I think it was an ad you guys had on Google. It was a blessing though; I tell you for sure.

"I asked my wife, 'What was it that attracted you to me on Christian Filipina? And she said 'It was not only the pictures you posted, but it was your heartfelt and true profile. You said what you were looking for. You were completely honest. You also said that you were almost a victim.' I almost fell victim to a scammer on another website," Alex explains.

Desiree elaborated on why she chose Alex: "I think we have this kind of compatibility when it comes to having common ideals or common principles. There was an instant chemistry. It's like there's electricity that came, or fired up; then I realized that I am totally in love with this person and that I really want to spend the rest of my life with him."

"At the end of the day it wasn't about how much they charged per month; it was about the results, and you guys definitely delivered the results!" Alex said appreciatively. "Thank you for having such a site and giving people the opportunity to find the love of their lifetime. I know one person who is interested in finding a Filipina girl and I will recommend to him your site. I will tell my friends, 'You know what? If you guys can't find love here in Toronto or in Canada, then expand your horizons!'"

"Christian Filipina wants to encourage its members. The

members are actually Christians. They are God-fearing people and they have this kind of faith in God. Have faith and God will do everything. If they allow God to manipulate their lives and pray hard for whatever they wish for, surely it will happen. It will be given to them by God. So the main point here is, you do not need to give up," advised Desiree. "For those who are really hoping to find the perfect match, just wait and wait and have patience and ask, or pray very, very hard; patience and prayer. There is really someone for them, a soul mate for them. In time, God's perfect time, he or she will meet them for eternity."

Was it a Sign?

"He has this kind of personality wherein he is really approachable," Desiree said about Alex. "He is very friendly. He is generous, thoughtful, all of those characteristics or traits. I really love his personality."

"I found out that she was the one during the summer last year," said Alex. "To some it might be surprising, but I knew it way before I first came to the Philippines just by talking to her. You would be surprised how much you can find out about each other through Skype rather than email and stuff like that. When you talk to each other you get to know each other on a deeper level."

"I don't know if this is a kind of a miracle when I knew Alex was to be my husband," confided Desiree. "I actually prayed hard, asking for a sign. I don't know if it was really a sign that came from Heaven, but I was inside the room praying hard that hopefully he was the one, and a butterfly came into my room. She is saying, 'This is the right decision for you to make. This is the right man for you to settle with,' and I assume that because it was the sign I asked for from my sister. So I am really overwhelmed with this site, Christian Filipina, because it is really heaven sent."

As They Say in Movies, an Adorable "Meet Cute"

"It is like the exact moment that I usually watch, when I see this kind of scene in movies," said Desiree excitedly, "where a guy or a woman approaches someone, meets for the first time and has a bond or connection. It's just a mix of emotions! I am just really excited to see him. At the same time and I am feeling really nervous. He might not like me! It was like an overwhelming joy, love, kind of feeling."

Talking about the first time he met Desiree, Alex said, "I'll be honest with you. I was a bit nervous, the fact that it was a different country. But I was not feeling as nervous as she was, she told me later. I spoke to her enough on Skype, I spoke enough to her family, but meeting in person is a bit more nerve wracking! But I kind of felt confident; standing strong on my feet. The first reaction, you don't know, should you kiss? Should you hug? For me it was a good, confident, first time meeting."

"The first or second day we mostly spent at home, most of the time we were with the family, really, more family, family! We were visiting a lot of relatives. I was there like on a display! Like the Statue of Liberty that the tourists were coming to see! Going to Momma's relatives, going to Papa's relatives, going to different places!

"'I became to them sort of son,' she told me her momma said. It was very touching. I could relate; my grandfather passed away last year and her oldest sister passed away and they felt very empty. They never had a son; only three daughters. When she told me, it was heartfelt, touching," Alex sighed emotionally. "'Like an angel' she said, 'You know you kind of filled the gap of emptiness, of sorrow. You are like God's gift to us!' When I heard that, I was speechless. I felt exactly the same way. I felt always stressed. I felt not in my own place. I couldn't find anyone to truly love me for who I am as a person. So, you know, the feeling was mutual."

"Definitely, they love Alex," confirmed Desiree. "It's like they have known him for several years."

"Don't Wait to Propose!"

"We arrived at their house and I proposed that same night when we were unpacking. My dad told me, 'Wait,' and my mom said, 'No, don't wait!' and I thought, 'Yeah, that's exactly what I want to do.' So I proposed to her."

Alex and Desiree were married October 4, 2013. "We had a low profile wedding, her family, Momma, Papa, sister and neighbors were witnesses. We had it in the city hall of San Fernando, in the office of the Mayor. He was the solemnizing officer at our wedding. We just dressed in plain clothes then we went to Shanghai Palace and had dinner." Alex's friend told him, "It makes more sense than spending thousands and thousands of dollars for that kind of thing even though it's special. Leave that money where you guys can go to honeymoon or buy something nice after, like a car, or something else." "We had a low profile wedding; nothing fancy considering also that both of us were very, very physically sick. I had a recurring fever. My poor Baby, she got sick too because she was taking care of me. We were 'fake happy' during our ceremony! We had to be, but in reality we were burning up," Alex said. "Poor girl was caring for me like I was a big, sick baby! I felt bad for her; she was caring for me day and night, night and day!

Immigration Delays Mean Long Distance Relationships

"I did sponsorship for her," Alex explained. It's basically the same thing as an Immigrant Visa for a spouse in the United States. "It's a permanent visa, so when she came, she became a permanent resident, the step before becoming a citizen. The only things she cannot do are vote and have a passport, yet. We actually used the help of the local Member of Provincial Parliament in Toronto to fill out the personal information and disclosure. They said six to nine months.

"The unfortunate part is that the Canadian, United States side is very easy, but when it comes to the Manila side it's a bit long," said Alex. "I know why now; somebody told me that there are a lot of arranged marriages, a lot of scams and fraud, so that's why they have to scan through all the things and make sure they are all valid. It also depends on the office, on how backlogged they are. All these reasons are valid, but still it's frustrating, I waited for her for a long time. We were in the same boat like everyone else."

"It was difficult; long distance relationships require two people's commitments," Alex learned. "For the sake of my wife, I was ready to wait as long as necessary. We both knew that that's the disadvantage. But you know what? I had to look outside the box; so I was prepared for that."

Desiree explained further, "We kinda' set up a plan where we really took time to communicate with each other every day as much as possible. We had to see each other every day, even if we are busy. Patience is a virtue," Desiree added. "You need patience in your heart. There is a saying that goes, 'If you are waiting for someone who is really worth the wait, then that is true love.'"

Building a New Future

"My best friend said that it's very good to open up a business in the Philippines. I have some money saved and I'm thinking to work here a year or two and save up and all of us open a business there. Quite frankly, I love Canada; it's a great country, but the weather here is unbearable, seven months of being cold; it's too extreme! So that's the reason why I want to live somewhere else other than Canada during the winter. Philippines I love, because the people are nice, the people are sweet, climate is good. Even though in the beginning for a white guy like me, it was hot," Alex laughed, "but I settled in pretty well. They live in a suburban area away from the city. Manila is a crazy city to live in, but they live in a little village; that is nice."

Alex and Desiree are thinking of "maybe building an apartment building and renting it to folks that cannot afford much. Plus her papa has a mango farm; maybe thinking about something like that. The possibilities are endless," said Alex. "You have to weigh the options and consider the possibilities and figure what is most profitable.

"So, most likely, we will live in my parent's house for now," in Toronto, said Alex, "and maybe rent a place, but we aren't thinking about any permanent settling yet. The future plans haven't been solidified."

Desiree is focusing on the big picture: "It's just a plan, but what's the most important thing is we are together. I really want to be with him no matter what the place is, as long as I am with him forever."

When asked about wanting children, Alex answered, "If you marry in any other country, no one asks, but there was a question on the pre-marriage counseling form; 'How many children do you want to have?' And I was like, 'What should I put? Should I put three? Should I put 12?'" he laughed. "One thing I do know, my parents-in-law would like to have a boy in their family, but for me, I told them, 'Look, I don't care, boy, girl, twins, triplets, quadruplets, octuplets; it doesn't matter! What matters is that both wife and the baby are safe and sound and, most importantly, healthy. It doesn't matter who, when, where, and how many, but ideally the number would be three, I guess; we'll see how it goes."

"Of course, we are dreaming of having a baby boy or baby girl, in time," Desiree said shyly. "We really have a plan of building our own family."

"A lot of people have been asking me, 'How come you don't have kids?' I said, 'Look, we were only together three weeks! You know what, we weren't concentrating on that! We were getting to know each other on a deeper level, getting to know the family, the relatives, plus marriage ceremonies; all these things! So three weeks kinda' went by really fast." Alex laughed, "Obviously there will come a time for making babies!" now that Desiree has finally arrived in Canada.

"Hopefully our successful love story will serve as an inspiration to others! Thank you for inviting us to do this kind of interview; for sure we will inspire others," believes Desiree. "Hopefully they will also have a happy ending like our fairy tale that came true for us."

Priceless Opportunity for Christian Single Men
Who Are Resolved to Be Successful...

Claim your FREE
INTERNATIONAL ROMANCE
BONUS PACK

jam-packed with everything you need to be
successful this year.

Your FREE GIFT INCLUDES:

3. International Romance Success Workshop Online Access

Experience this once-in-a-lifetime One Day Workshop with Peter
Christopher, author of "How to Meet, Date and Marry Your Filipina
Wife." This access is over a $397 value, complete with video recordings
and workshop downloads. In will help you learn exactly how to go about
online dating and how to plan for a possible trip and relationship.

2. A copy of "How to Meet, Date and Marry Your Filipina Wife"

We'll rush you a copy of Christian Filipina founder Peter Christopher's
ultimate handbook to ensure your safety and success.

3. Free Romance Consultation

Receive a certificate for a complimentary 15-minute consultation with
one of our trained Romance Consultants, to help you answer any
questions you have on your mind:

IVY   ALVIE   MARILYN   GLAIZA   JARETTE

There is a one-time charge of $5.95 to cover shipping and handling of your FREE gift.

To claim your free gift, simply call us at 800-578-1469 or go to
www.ChristianFilipina.com/freegift

Made in the USA
Middletown, DE
24 February 2023

25525631R00038